JOBS IN THE AIR FORCE

by Emma Huddleston

Minneapolis, Minnesota

Credits
Cover and title page, © Airubon/iStock, © Senior Airman Bobby Cummings/Wikimedia Commons, and © aappp/Shutterstock; 5T, © Senior Airman Ryan Conroy/U. S. Air Force; 5B, © Staff Sgt. Rose Gudex/DVIDS; 7, © Bettmann/Getty Images; 8–9, © Uber Bilder/Alamy Stock Photo; 11T, © Tech. Sgt. Alexander Cook/DVIDS; 11B, © Staff Sgt. Micaiah Anthony/DVIDS; 13T, © Airman 1st Class Daniel Farrell/DVIDS; 13B, © Airman 1st Class Eugene Oliver/DVIDS; 15T, © Staff Sgt. John Bainter/DVIDS; 15B, © Senior Master Sgt. Paul Holcomb/DVIDS; 17T, © Staff Sgt. Austin Siegel/DVIDS; 17B, © Airman 1st Class Courtney Sebastianelli/DVIDS; 19, © Brian G. Rhodes/DVIDS; 21T, © Airman Anabel Del Valle/DVIDS; 21B, © GE Global Research/DVIDS; 23, © Senior Airman Jeffrey Parkinson/DVIDS; 25, © Tech. Sgt. Anthony Nelson/DVIDS; 26–27, © Staff Sgt. Justin Parsons/DVIDS; 28, © U. S. Air Force/Wikimedia Commons; 29, © Staff Sgt. Nathanael Callon/DVIDS, © Staff Sgt. Devin Doskey/DVIDS, © SHARKY PHOTOGRAPHY/Adobe Stock, and © Dontstop/iStock.

Bearport Publishing Company Product Development Team
President: Jen Jenson; Director of Product Development: Spencer Brinker; Managing Editor: Allison Juda; Associate Editor: Naomi Reich; Associate Editor: Tiana Tran; Art Director: Colin O'Dea; Designer: Kim Jones; Designer: Kayla Eggert; Product Development Assistant: Owen Hamlin

Statement on Usage of Generative Artificial Intelligence
Bearport Publishing remains committed to publishing high-quality nonfiction books. Therefore, we restrict the use of generative AI to ensure accuracy of all text and visual components pertaining to a book's subject. See BearportPublishing.com for details.

Library of Congress Cataloging-in-Publication Data

Names: Huddleston, Emma, author.
Title: Jobs in the Air Force / by Emma Huddleston.
Description: Minneapolis, Minnesota : Bearport Publishing Company, [2025] | Series: Military careers | Includes bibliographical references and index.
Identifiers: LCCN 2024007952 (print) | LCCN 2024007953 (ebook) | ISBN 9798892320368 (library binding) | ISBN 9798892321693 (ebook)
Subjects: LCSH: United States. Air Force--Vocational guidance--Juvenile literature. | United States. Air Force--Juvenile literature.
Classification: LCC UG633 .H8183 2025 (print) | LCC UG633 (ebook) | DDC 358.40023--dc23/eng/20240220
LC record available at https://lccn.loc.gov/2024007952
LC ebook record available at https://lccn.loc.gov/2024007953

Copyright © 2025 Bearport Publishing Company. All rights reserved. No part of this publication may be reproduced in whole or in part, stored in any retrieval system, or transmitted in any form or by any means, electronic, mechanical, photocopying, recording, or otherwise, without written permission from the publisher. Bearport Publishing is a division of Chrysalis Education Group.

For more information, write to Bearport Publishing, 5357 Penn Avenue South, Minneapolis, MN 55419.

CONTENTS

Undercover 4
History of the Air Force 6
Joining the Air Force 10
Masters of Flight........................14
In and Out 18
Engineering for the Future 20
Working on a Team.....................22
Outer Space............................24
Community of Care 26

More about the Air Force 28
Glossary.................................. 30
Read More................................. 31
Learn More Online....................... 31
Index..................................... 32
About the Author 32

UNDERCOVER

The leaves of a bush move—only this isn't really a plant at all. It is a member of the United States Air Force camouflaged to stay out of sight. The special **reconnaissance** airman is deep behind enemy lines, gathering **intelligence** about what the opposition is doing. They are setting up **infrastructure**.

The success of future **missions** depends on the hidden airman. With the information the special reconnaissance airman brings back, the air force can move into enemy territory quickly. This is just one of the many important jobs in the United States Air Force.

CAREER SPOTLIGHT: Special Reconnaissance Airman

Job Requirements:
- 17 to 42 years old
- 6 months specialized training
- Enlisted

Skills and Training:

 Battlefield Awareness

 Identification & Strategy

 Weapons Operation

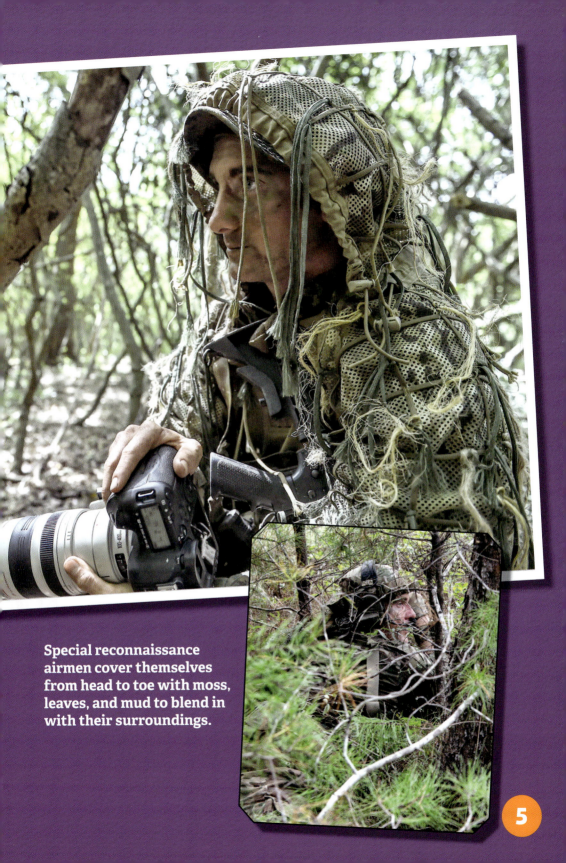

Special reconnaissance airmen cover themselves from head to toe with moss, leaves, and mud to blend in with their surroundings.

HISTORY OF THE AIR FORCE

The United States military first used aircraft for battle during World War I (1914–1918). Though it would be years until an air force was its own military branch, flying soon became an important part of the war. Aircraft were mainly used for gathering information near enemy lines.

But when planes were finally used for **combat**, they changed the way wars were fought forever. Soldiers flew planes to shoot down enemy aircraft. They used planes to drop bombs on targets down below. The atomic bombs that eventually brought World War II (1939–1945) to a close were dropped from aircraft.

> From planes, pilots could see battlefields and plan where to send troops. Aircraft helped carry people and supplies long distances.

Soldiers who flew aircraft were part of the United States Army during World War I.

It wasn't until 1947 that the United States Air Force became its own military branch. Today, members of the air force do different work during war and peacetime. When there is war, members fly aircraft to help ground crews in battle. They are also used to recover downed airmen from behind enemy lines.

During peacetime, the air force focuses on strengthening the U.S. military with aircraft technology. They are working hard to make even stronger and faster aircraft, such as jets and **drones**. Air force crews may be sent to areas all over the world to drop off food, resources, and medical supplies for people in need.

An air force drone

★ ★ ★ ★ ★ ★ ★ ★ ★

Drones are flown without a pilot inside. Instead, they are controlled from far away by a person or directed by a navigation program.

JOINING THE AIR FORCE

The first step to becoming an **enlisted** airman is going through basic training, or boot camp. This intensive course lasts seven and a half weeks. At the beginning, **recruits** focus on building endurance and learning air force rules.

Physical conditioning starts at 5 a.m. each morning. Most of the day is spent doing drills, such as running several miles and crawling while holding a weapon. Recruits practice **martial arts** for battle in the **field**. They also learn how to use and maintain weapons.

★ ★ ★ ★ ★ ★ ★ ★ ★

The lowest rank of the air force is enlisted airmen. Higher-ranking members are called officers. They are the ones who plan, lead, and assign enlisted airmen on missions.

Getting into top physical shape is one of the goals of basic training.

Toward the end of boot camp, recruits take the PACER FORGE test. In it, they are split into teams to complete several combat **simulations** over a period of 36 hours. Instructors act as enemies, forcing recruits to make decisions quickly just as they would have to in actual battle. Recruits practice facing difficult challenges, such as avoiding enemy fire, walking across land containing hidden explosives, and rescuing a downed airman in under three minutes.

After basic training, most enlisted airmen go on to do more **specialized** training. They can choose among more than 200 jobs within the United States Air Force.

★ ★ ★ ★ ★ ★ ★ ★ ★

Most airmen serve active duty, where they work for the military full-time. Some work part-time as part of the Air Force Reserve. These soldiers serve the military while also living a **civilian** life.

Air force recruits practice rescuing downed airmen using mannequins.

MASTERS OF FLIGHT

Some members of the air force serve in the skies. Air force pilots fly some of the most advanced aircraft in the world. Each pilot specializes in a specific aircraft. Remotely piloted airplane pilots fly drones to places that might be too risky for human pilots. They gather **satellite** images of enemy troops or bases to share with officers in the field. This helps the air force plan strike missions. Remotely piloted airplane pilots also control weapon systems—**deploying** missiles, rockets, and bombs during combat.

CAREER SPOTLIGHT: Remotely Piloted Airplane Pilot

Job Requirements:
- 18 to 40 years old
- 8.5 weeks officer training
- Officer

Skills and Training:
- Air Support
- Surveillance & Reconnaissance
- Weapons Operation

Combat systems officers specialize in navigation, aircraft technology, and weapon systems. They help pilots move through difficult places, such as mountainous regions. These officers also perform electronic warfare, blocking and jamming radio signals to keep the enemy from communicating with one another.

Aircraft armament systems specialists test and maintain weapons. They make sure explosives, missiles, and other weapons are set up and ready to launch. This helps make sure pilots have all their weapons prepared to fire.

CAREER SPOTLIGHT: Aircraft Armament Systems Specialist

Job Requirements:
- 17 to 42 years old
- 7.5 weeks training
- Enlisted

Skills and Training:
-  Tracking & Navigation
-  Weapons Maintenance & Operation
- Physical Strength

Aircraft armament systems specialists have to keep weapons ready at all times in case of emergencies.

IN AND OUT

In addition to combat jobs, the air force also has search and rescue teams. Survival, evasion, resistance, and escape specialists prepare rescue crews to recover injured or captured airmen from behind enemy lines. These specialists plan in advance of the mission. Combat rescue officers are those physically leading the missions. These officers decide the best ways to get in and out of places without the team being noticed or caught themselves.

CAREER SPOTLIGHT: Combat Rescue Officer

Job Requirements:
- 18 to 41 years old
- 9.5 weeks officer training
- Officer

Skills and Training:
-  Day & Night Operations
-  Personnel Recovery
- Parachute Experts

Air force soldiers are trained to handle any type of situation out in the field.

ENGINEERING FOR THE FUTURE

Engineers and researchers in the air force design and build new technology that helps other airmen do their work. Civil engineers are primarily responsible for constructing and maintaining buildings. But they have also worked to develop robot dogs that can help detect harmful chemicals and gases.

Other air force engineers design shirts and patches that airmen can wear while training and when out on missions. This wearable technology helps monitor heart rate, blood flow, and other health markers to keep airmen safe during intense situations.

CAREER SPOTLIGHT: Civil Engineer

Job Requirements:
- 18 to 42 years old
- 8.5 weeks officer training
- Officer

Skills and Training:
- Construction Management
- Combat Operations Support
- Disaster Preparedness

Robot dogs can search dangerous areas while airmen remain at a safe distance.

21

WORKING ON A TEAM

Getting aircraft from one place to another takes teamwork. Radar, airfield & weather systems specialists install and maintain radios and weather monitors on aircraft. Air traffic controllers use the radios to guide pilots during takeoff and landing, as well as manage aircraft coming into and out of the base. They work in control towers to monitor flights and weather. Air traffic controllers communicate with pilots about flight paths and warn of difficult weather. This helps keep everyone safe while they complete their missions.

CAREER SPOTLIGHT: Radar, Airfield & Weather Systems Specialist

Job Requirements:
- 17 to 42 years old
- 7.5 weeks training
- Enlisted

Skills and Training:
 Construction Management
 Combat Operations Support
 Disaster Preparedness

OUTER SPACE

Some airmen even work on technology for outer space. Space operations officers are in charge of satellite programs for navigation and **surveillance**. These officers track **debris** orbiting Earth to make sure it avoids satellites. They are developing new space technology, such as reusable spacecraft that can bring wireless energy to remote locations.

Space system operations specialists detect and keep track of missile launches. They also help with rocket launches and other space operations. Sometimes, airmen work with members of the U.S. Space Force. Together, these two military branches protect and repair **GPS** systems.

CAREER SPOTLIGHT: Space Operations Officer

Job Requirements:
- 18 to 42 years old
- 8.5 weeks officer training
- Officer

Skills and Training:
- Space Surveillance
- Communication & Tracking
- Satellite Operations

COMMUNITY OF CARE

Many jobs in the air force are a lot like those in civilian life, but with a military twist. Some jobs have to be done in the air. Flight nurses, for example, give medical care to airmen onboard aircraft.

The United States Air Force has many different careers. All these jobs help create a strong combat and support system for the military. From the ground, to the skies, and even up into outer space, dedicated airmen work together to protect the country.

★ ★ ★ ★ ★ ★ ★ ★ ★

In under 100 days, air force medical specialists created a special container to safely transport people with COVID-19.

The COVID-19 shipping container had safety seats and seat belts for passengers to strap themselves in as they are moved.

MORE ABOUT THE AIR FORCE

AT A GLANCE

Founded: July 26, 1947
Membership: More than 300,000
Categories of ranks: Enlisted airman, officer
Largest base: Eglin Air Force Base in Florida

DID YOU KNOW?

★ In 1980, 97 women from the first female class graduated from the Air Force Academy.

★ General Charles Q. Brown Jr. is the first black Chief of Staff of the Air Force.

★ The bald eagle is a symbol of the Air Force because it is known for striking powerfully from the air.

General Charles Q. Brown Jr.

GLOSSARY

civilian a person who is not in the military

combat fighting or having to do with fighting between people or armies

debris scattered pieces of something that has been wrecked or destroyed

deploying sending to an area for a specific purpose

drones airplanes without pilots that are flown by remote control

enlisted soldiers who have joined a branch of the armed forces without prior special training and hold ranks below officers

field in the military, a place where battles are fought

GPS a system that uses satellites to give location information

infrastructure buildings used for military purposes

intelligence in war, information about a possible enemy or area

martial arts styles of fighting or self-defense

missions jobs that have a particular task or goal

reconnaissance a military activity where soldiers are sent to gather information about something

recruits people who are going through the process of joining the armed forces

satellite a spacecraft that circles the planet to gather information and send it back to Earth

simulations training activities made to look or feel real

specialized focused on one subject or area of work

surveillance the close watch of a person or group's activities

READ MORE

Chandler, Matt. *Drones (Torque: Military Science).* Minneapolis: Bellwether Media, 2022.

Morey, Allan. *U.S. Air Force (U.S. Armed Forces).* Minneapolis: Jump!, 2021.

Ventura, Marne. *U.S. Air Force (U.S. Armed Forces).* Minneapolis: Kaleidoscope, 2023.

LEARN MORE ONLINE

1. Go to **www.factsurfer.com** or scan the QR code below.
2. Enter "**Air Force Jobs**" into the search box.
3. Click on the cover of this book to see a list of websites.

INDEX

aircraft 6–9, 14, 16–17, 22, 26
basic training 10–12
civilian 12, 26
combat 6, 12, 14, 16, 18, 20, 22, 26
drone 9, 14–15
engineer 20
enlisted 4, 10, 12, 16, 22, 28
GPS 24
intelligence 4
medical 9, 26–27
missions 4, 10, 14, 18, 20, 22
officer 10, 14, 16, 18, 20, 24, 28
pilot 9, 14, 16, 22
recruits 10, 12–13
researcher 20
robot 20–21
specialist 16–18, 22, 24, 27
satellite 14, 24
space 24, 26
weather 22

ABOUT THE AUTHOR

Emma Huddleston lives with her family in the Twin Cities. She enjoys reading, taking walks, and swing dancing. To all those who serve in the military, she says thank you!